I0213357

The Recipe for a Happy Marriage

(For Dina and Jonah Pawley)

By
Sheryl and Tom Freeman
(and a whole lot of other people who
care about you!)

Contents

Appetizers/Drinks/Soups/Salads

Main Dishes

Desserts

Recipe for a Happy Marriage

Ingredients

4 cups of love
2 cups of loyalty
3 cups of forgiveness
3 cups of friendship
5 spoons of hope
2 spoons of tenderness
1 barrel of laughter

1. Mix love and loyalty.
2. Blend it with tenderness, kindness, and understanding.
3. Add friendship and hope, and sprinkle abundantly with laughter.
4. Garnish with hugs and kisses.
5. Serve generous helpings daily.

Appetizers/Drinks/
Soups/Salads

Having a lot of money early in a marriage is not all that important. Don't compare your lives with other people. Appreciate each other and count your blessings. Be each other's best friend!

- Nana and Papa (Jonah's grandparents)

Still happily married after 58 years!

Fruit Dip – Devonshire Cream

By Nana and Papa

Ingredients

1 cup whipping cream
¼ cup powdered sugar
1 cup sour cream
¼ cup granulated sugar
1-ounce triple sec (optional)
1 tsp. fresh squeezed lemon juice

1. Whip cream with powdered sugar until stiff.
2. Fold in sour cream, granulated sugar, triple sec, and lemon juice.

   Keep cold until serving time.

Veggie Dip

Ingredients

1 cup mayo
2 cups sour cream
1 cup cream cheese
1 tsp. lemon juice

1. Combine ingredients, mixing well.
2. Cover tightly and refrigerate.

The Bible says "Do not let the sun go down on your anger." Ephesians 4:26. In a marriage, this essentially means do not go to bed angry. However, we have found that sometimes it is necessary to go to bed instead of arguing fruitlessly at an impasse. The next day is a new day to approach the disagreement with a new perspective and ready to find a mutual understanding and resolution. Also, when you experience frustration with your partner, have the courage and integrity to take an honest look within yourself and discover where you may be wrong, too, and apologize.

Laura Pawley, Jonah's mom ♥

Tomato Basil Squares
By Laura Pawley

Great appetizer! Fresh basil makes it even more delicious!

Ingredients

1 10 oz package of refrigerated pizza crust
2 cups shredded mozzarella cheese, divided
¼ cup fresh Parmesan cheese, grated
2 tbsp. fresh basil leaves, snipped, or 2 tsp. dried basil leaves
2/3 cup mayonnaise
1 garlic clove, pressed
4 Roma tomatoes, thinly sliced

1. Preheat oven to 375 degrees.
2. Roll out pizza crust onto a lightly greased 12x15 cookie sheet or baking stone and press to within 1 inch of the edge. (My cookie sheet has a raised edge. I go all the way to it.)
3. Bake for 5 minutes. Sprinkle crust with 1 cup mozzarella cheese. Set aside.
4. In a medium bowl, combine the remaining 1 cup of mozzarella cheese, Parmesan cheese, basil, mayonnaise, and garlic. Mix well.
5. Slice tomatoes thinly and arrange in a single layer over mozzarella cheese on the crust.
6. Drop the cheese mixture onto the tomatoes with a spoon and spread with a rubber spatula to cover evenly.
7. Bake 15-20 minutes or until the top is golden brown and bubbly.
8. Cut into squares and serve warm.

Cook for each other. It can be a great meal or just drinks and apps. It is the language of love that never grows old.

- Emily Payne and Eddy Polon, cousins on Brian's side.

Pico De Gallo Salsa

By Emily Payne and Eddy Polon

Yield: About 2 cups

Ingredients

2 tablespoons diced onion
2 cups tomatoes chopped into ¼ inch cubes
1 serrano chile, finely chopped
2 tablespoons finely chopped cilantro
1 teaspoon sugar
¼ cup Mexican beer
1 teaspoon salt
Juice of 1 lime

1. Put the onion in a strainer, rinse with hot water, and drain.
2. Combine all ingredients and mix well.
3. Let sit in the refrigerator for at least 30 minutes before serving.
4. Feel free to consume the rest of the beer while waiting.

Note: More sugar may be used if the tomatoes are acidic, but make sure the salsa does not taste of sugar.

Our note: Emily always mixes the drinks, and Eddy makes the salsa. We open a bag of Trader Joe's tortilla chips (white corn), make a toast (always make a toast!), and.... whatever we have planned next will inevitably be more fun.

Margaritas

By Emily Payne and Eddy Polon

Ingredients

Ice cubes
2 measures tequila
1/14 measures triple sec or Cointreau
¾ measure lime juice (or lemon if preferred)
Lime wedge

For a Pitcher (14 margaritas)
3 cups + 4 ounces tequila
2 cups + 1 ½ ounces triple sec
1 cup + 2 ½ ounces lime juice

1. Rub the rim of the glass with a wedge of lime and dip the rim into a saucer of salt.
2. Half-fill the shaker with ice cubes.
3. Pour in the lime juice, triple sec or Cointreau, and tequila.
4. Shake well and strain into the champagne saucer.
5. Garnish with a wedge of lime on the edge of the glass.

Showering with Loving Advice

As I sit watching TV and doing my crossword puzzle,
it's a good time to free my creative brain from formal
muzzle.
After 55 years of marriage, I should be full of Golden Rules,
And be able to offer you great marital tools.

So, what words of loving advice would be helpful to hear?
What sweet sayings should I be pouring in your ear?
Seriously, you should use humor, whenever you can.
Of gratitude, patience, and kind tones, I'm a big fan.

Mostly believe in yourself because you have what it takes.
You have an excellent moral compass, for blessings' sakes.
You are creative and can see things from multiple angles.
Use these gifts whenever you need untangles.

We glory in the light shining from your love.
Wishing you and Jonah long life together and Mazal Tov!

• Omi

Linda's Chicken Soup and Matzoh Balls

By Omi

Ingredients

Two Whole chickens cut up (including necks)
2 carrots
2 stalks celery
1 big peeled onion (cut up)
2 cloves garlic sliced
1 leek
1 bay leaf
1 parsnip
1 handful parsley

1. Using a 16-quart pot, bring water to within 3 inches of the top
2. Add the chicken
3. Bring to a boil. Skim off beige gunk
4. Add the vegetables (cleaned, peeled, sliced, quartered, and chopped as needed)
5. Add salt and pepper to taste
6. Cook overnight if possible

Matzoh Balls
By Omi

Ingredients

12 eggs
2 cups of Matzoh meal
1 teaspoon Lawry's

1. Beat the egg whites, and then slowly blend in mixed yolks of eggs.
2. Fold in matzoh meal and salt
3. Let stand for 5 minutes.
4. Form balls and drop them into boiling water.
5. Cook for at least 45 minutes.
6. The mixture should be loose, not stiff. Form matzoh balls with help of a greased spoon.

Laugh Your Way to a Better Marriage - Mark Gungor. Make it a priority to find and attend this marriage seminar. It is by far the best we ever attended and makes sense to both husbands and wives. It is simple and understandable and entertaining and engaging!

Do the simple, little home tasks for her before she asks you to. Especially after kids come. Don't ever ask her why the dishes didn't get done after she spent the whole day at home with the kids and you worked all day.

- Harley C. Pawley, Jonah's dad

COLD KICKIN' CHICKEN COUSCOUS SOUP

By Harley C. Pawley

This is easy, fast, and delicious to prepare! Nothing is better than chicken soup for a cold, and the turmeric, lemongrass, and ginger help fight it off.

Ingredients

1 cup chopped onion (about ½ of a medium)
¾-1 cup sliced leek (about 1 medium, white and light green parts only)
½ cup sliced carrots
½ cup chopped celery
1 tablespoon minced ginger or ginger paste
1 tablespoon minced lemongrass or paste
2 cloves minced garlic
½ teaspoon ground turmeric
4 cups chicken stock
2 cups cooked chicken, chopped or shredded (rotisserie chicken is great)
½ cup pearl couscous
lemon cut in half
salt and pepper
chopped fresh parsley for garnish, if desired

1. Heat one tablespoon oil in a 4-5 quart Dutch oven or stock pot over medium heat. When hot, add onions, leeks, carrots and celery. Saute until the vegetables are soft, about 6 minutes. Stir in the ginger, lemongrass, and garlic and heat until aromatic. Sprinkle the turmeric over the vegetables and stir.

2. Add the stock, chicken and couscous, and bring to a light boil. Cover, reduce heat to maintain a gentle simmer, cook for 15 minutes. Squeeze the half lemon into the soup, taste, and season with salt and pepper to your liking. Top with parsley if desired before serving.

Make your partner feel as special as they did when you met them. Never take them for granted, and always appreciate them. Do little things for them (like you did when you met), and when they do things for you, notice them, and always let them know how much you appreciate it.

- Mark and Lorie Borges

Harvest Bisque

By Mark and Lorie Burges

Ingredients

1 pound of butternut squash
5 cups of chicken stock
4 tablespoons butter
4 tablespoons flour
1 teaspoon curry powder
¾ cup half and half (I use milk)
1 tablespoon lime juice
½ teaspoon salt
¼ teaspoon white pepper

1. Peel seed and cut the squash into 1-inch cubes. Place a in heavy, 4-quart pot with chicken stock.
2. Cook over medium heat until tender, about 15 minutes.
3. Using a slotted spoon, transfer squash to a blender or food processor. Blend until smooth. Stir the stock into squash puree. Set aside.
4. In the same pot, melt butter; stir in flour and curry.
5. Cook, stirring, over medium heat until smooth.
6. Add pureed squash mixture to a pot. Increase heat to medium-high and stir until soup thickens slightly.
7. Reduce heat and add half and half. Do not allow the soup to boil after this point.
8. Add lime juice, salt, and white pepper. Ladle soup into serving bowls, garnish with lime, and serve immediately.

Southwestern Chili

By Mark and Lorie Burges

Ingredients

1 tbsp vegetable oil
1 cup chopped onion
1 can chopped green chilies
1 ½ tsp. ground cumin
¼ tsp. ground cloves
1/8 tsp. Sage
2 cans of great northern or white kidney beans
2 cans (14oz.) chicken broth
3 cups cooked chicken
2 cloves garlic, chopped

1. Saute onion, chilies and spices in large, heavy pot.
2. Stir in beans, broth, chicken and garlic. Bring to boil.
3. Reduce heat and simmer 50-60 minutes uncovered.
4. Garnish with chopped avocado and sour cream or shredded Monterey Jack Cheese.

Noteworthy Nibbles of Nice Nuggets for Newlyweds After Nuptials

Accept Your Partner the Way They Are

That doesn't mean you can't help each other create better habits, though. Part of a good marriage is learning and growing together. So, if one of you finds a certain behavior annoying, work together to discuss it and come to an understanding.

Always Support One Another

While you might not always agree, make sure never to put each other down or bicker in front of your friends, family, or work colleagues. You should always have each other's back in public and save the disagreements for behind closed doors.

Argue, but Argue Healthily

Arguments are inevitable in any relationship, be it marriage, family dynamic, or friendship. But how you handle disagreements with your partner will ultimately determine a great amount of happiness in your marriage. It's important to fight fairly when points of contention come up. Ditch the blame game, and do not use an argument as an excuse to be rude or disrespectful. Always remember that disagreements are momentary in the span of your lives together!

Check-In with Each Other

Don't forget to check in on your partner to see how they are doing in all the hustle and bustle of daily life. Make sure their needs are being met and see how their day has been. Don't neglect to regularly ask yourself, "how can I be a better spouse?" and mean it!

Discuss Finances and Budgets

Make sure always to be open and honest about the monetary aspect of your shared lives. Now that both of you are joined in marriage, the financial considerations will be doubled.

Money is one of the most significant marriage stressors, so make time to sit down and talk about your finances together and work out a budget that both of you can follow. Don't keep spending secrets from your partner—transparency is vital in marriage and money.

Don't Sweat the Small Stuff

A quintessential bit of advice is to not worry too much about the minor details. Ask yourself if it is worth stressing about—will it even matter tomorrow? By all means, if something is bothering you, speak up; but don't sweat the small stuff.

Say "I Love You"
You can never say "I love you" too much! Even after years of being together, it's essential not to lose that spark you have with your partner. Let them know what you love about them and give them your love every day.
Send texts with kisses or leave romantic notes in their bag to let your partner know how much you care, and give them a pleasant little surprise during the day when they see the notes!

Set Long Term Goals
Plan for your future together and promote teamwork when you set long-term goals. It will give you a good sense of where your marriage is going and what the future might look like for both of you.
Setting future goals is an exciting step in a new marriage and gives you both a sense of shared achievement!

Share Memories
Creating memories together is important for a healthy and happy marriage. But you should also revisit the special times you already have had. Share the memories of dating, being engaged, and getting married—reminisce about these times together. The time has come for you and your newlywed to start the rest of your lives together. Whether you plan to travel the world or settle down and have kids, there are steps you should take to ensure a long and happy marriage together.

Have Realistic Expectations
It's important to enter your new marriage with realistic expectations for your partner, relationship, and the future. Don't expect your marriage to emulate anyone else's—be realistic with expectations, discuss them with your partner, and compromise.

-   Mom and Dad (Slipock)

MOM'S EASY ASIAN-STYLE CHICKEN SALAD

By Robin Slipock

Ingredients for Salad

4 diced cooked skinless boneless chicken breasts or thighs
1 1/4 cups bean sprouts
1 1/2 cups snow peas
1 1/2 cups red, yellow, and green diced bell peppers
1 1/2 cups sliced carrots
1 1/2 cups cabbage (red or green)
4 sprigs of sliced cilantro to taste
1/4 cup diced celery

Ingredients for Dressing

½ cup toasted sesame oil
1 tablespoon extra virgin olive oil
3 tablespoon rice vinegar
2 tablespoon light soy sauce or ponzu sauce
2 tablespoon maple syrup
1 tablespoon freshly squee zed lime juice
1 clove garlic (minced)
1 tablespoon grated ginger
1 teaspoon sriracha
1 teaspoon toasted sesame seeds

1. Combine all ingredients.
2. Serve chilled.

1. Always show each other respect. Even when you're fighting, you have to maintain respect for each other in order for things to work. It's important to keep calm when you have disagreements. It's OK to get angry, but never resort to name-calling or spiteful comments. I don't like being wrong, and even if I was wrong in the beginning, I don't want to be disrespectful and have to be wrong more than I already am!

2. In 10 years, when the dopamine has waned, remember: Life is a crazy ride. It's a privilege to go through it with a partner." — Kristen Bell

- Melanie and Greg Proden (cousin)

Mexican Grilled Chicken Salad

By Melanie and Greg Proden

Ingredients

1 pound boneless, skinless chicken breast
1 packet taco seasoning
2 heads of romaine lettuce
1 pint grape or cherry tomatoes, *halved*
2 avocados, *peeled and sliced*
1 cup fresh corn kernels
1 cup cooked crumbled bacon
1 bunch green onions, *chopped*
1/2 cup crumbled queso fresco cheese
1 cup thick ranch dressing, *from the refrigerated section tastes best, but regular works too*
1/2 cup fresh salsa

1. Preheat the grill to medium heat. Place the chicken breasts in a baking dish and sprinkle with Old El Paso Taco Seasoning. Turn to coat the chicken on all sides. Chop the lettuce and prepare all other vegetables.
2. Grill the chicken for 5 minutes per side. Then allow the chicken to rest for at least five minutes before slicing. Meanwhile, place the ranch dressing and the salsa in the blender and puree until smooth.
3. Pile the chopped lettuce on a large platter. Slice the chicken and arrange it over the lettuce. Then arrange the sliced avocados and tomatoes around the chicken. Sprinkle the corn, chopped green onions, crumbled bacon, and queso fresco over the entire salad. Serve immediately with a side of spicy tomato ranch dressing.

Value each other's differences, be supportive in each other's interests, and have fun. Don't let the things that matter least get in the way of the things that matter most.

-   Alan and Annette Briggs (Cousins)

Breadsticks

By Alan and Annette Briggs

Ingredients

1 ½ cups warm water (105-115 degrees F)
1 tbsp sugar
1 tbsp active dry yeast or bread machine yeast
½ tsp salt
3 – 4 ½ cups flour, divided

1. In a large mixing bowl, combine water, sugar, and yeast. Let stand for 10 minutes or until yeast is bubbly.
2. Add salt and stir. Add 1 ½ cups flour (may need up to 2 ½ cups depending on humidity and elevation) until dough starts to pull away from the sides of the bowl and it barely sticks to your finger.
3. Spray a glass or metal bowl with cooking spray and place dough in the bowl. Cover and let rise for 45 minutes or until doubled in bulk.
4. Remove from the bowl and place on a lightly floured surface. Spray a baking sheet with cooking spray. Roll dough into a rectangle 18 inches long and 9 inches wide and cut into 12 strips with a pizza cutter.
5. Roll out a piece of dough into a snake and then drape it over your forefinger and twist the dough. Place on baking sheet and repeat with 11 remaining pieces of dough. Try to space them evenly.
6. Cover the pan with a clean cloth and allow the dough to rise for another 30 minutes. When there is 15 minutes to go, preheat your over to 425 degrees F.
7. When the dough is done rising, bake for 10-12 minutes or until golden brown.
8. Rub some butter on top and sprinkle with garlic bread seasoning, or parmesan.

Homemade Pocket Sandwiches

By Alan and Annette Briggs

Ingredients

1 recipe breadstick dough
Desired fillings: about 6-8 ounces of deli meat and 4-8 ounces of shredded cheese

1. Prepare dough through the first rise. After dough has risen the first time, turn it into a lightly floured surface and roll into a rectangle 16 inches long and 8 inches wide. Using a pizza cutter, cut dough into 8 equal portions.
2. Leaving a little but of a margin on the right and left sides, add toppings, with the cheese going on last. Stretch the dough out a little to give yourself a bit more dough to work with. Fold the left side over the middle and the right side over that. Starting at the bottom of the "mummy," tightly roll the filled dough, stretching it very gently as you go to make sure you're getting a tight seal. Place on a sprayed cookie sheet and repeat with remaining dough.
3. When finished, cover the pan with a clean cloth and preheat your oven to 435 degrees F.
4. When oven has heated, bake pockets for about 15 minutes or until golden brown on top.
5. For shine, you could brush the tops with a bit of egg white mixed with water during the last 5 minutes of baking. Or, you could rub a little bit of butter on top of the rolls while they're still warm.

Main Dishes

Keep going on Friday night dates for years to come! Even when you have little ones. That's actually when you'll need them the most and when grandparents come in handy. 😀

-   Ric and Chris Lambert, friends of the Pawleys

Easy Chicken Parmesan

By Ric and Chris Lambert

Ingredients

4 chicken breast halves skinless boneless
½ cup all purpose flour
2 large eggs
⅔ cup Panko bread crumbs
⅔ cup Italian seasoning bread crumbs
⅓ cup parmesan cheese grated
2 tablespoons fresh parsley
4 tablespoons olive oil or as needed
24 ounces marinara sauce homemade or jarred
1 cup mozzarella cheese shredded
¼ cup Parmesan cheese shredded
1 teaspoon basil fresh, chopped, for garnish
1 teaspoon parsley fresh, chopped, for garnish

Instructions

1. Preheat the oven to 425°F.
2. Place the flour in a shallow bowl or dish. Place the eggs in a second shallow dish and beat with a fork.
3. In a third shallow dish, combine Panko, Italian seasoned crumbs, grated Parmesan, 2 tablespoons fresh parsley, ½ teaspoon salt, and ¼ teaspoon pepper.
4. Using a meat mallet, pound the chicken breasts to ½-inch thickness. After pounding, if they're very large, you can cut them in half. Pat the chicken dry with paper towels and season with ½ teaspoon salt and ¼ teaspoon black pepper.
5. Dip chicken into the flour and shake to remove any excess. Dip chicken in beaten eggs, then into the bread crumb mixture and gently press to adhere.
6. Preheat the oil over medium-high heat in a large skillet. Brown the chicken for about 2 minutes per side or until golden. It does not need to cook through.

7. In the bottom of a 9×13 baking dish, add 1 ½ cups of marinara sauce. Add the browned chicken. Top each piece of chicken with 2 tablespoons of marinara sauce in the center. Top with mozzarella and shredded parmesan.
8. Bake for 20-25 minutes or until golden and bubbly and the chicken reaches an internal temperature of 165°F with an instant-read thermometer.
9. Sprinkle with fresh herbs and serve over pasta.

Never mention the D word. Love is not just an emotion. It's also an action word of faith, hope, and living the journey of a lifetime.

- Mark & Rennie Ling – Pawley family friends ❤

Best Ever Applesauce Meatloaf

By Mark and Rennie Ling

Ingredients

1lb ground beef
1 raw egg
2 T chopped onion
Sea salt to taste
½ cup uncooked oats
½ cup applesauce
2T catsup or bbq sauce

1. Combine ingredients and mix well
2. Put in greased loaf pan
3. Add catsup or bbq sauce on top
4. Bake at 400 degrees for 40 minutes

Breathe and think before speaking when angry.

- Hope Lorimer - friend of family and lover of black cats 🐈

Salmon with Dill

By Hope Lorimer

Ingredients

4 tbsp unsalted butter
1 shallot minced
1 tbsp fresh dill minced
1 piece of salmon
1 lemon sliced thin
Salt and pepper

1. Adjust the oven rack to the middle and heat to 450 degrees.
2. Melt butter in a saucepan.
3. Add shallot, and 1/4 tsp salt, and cook until softened (1 min).
4. Take off the heat and stir in the dill.
5. Put foil in a pan, and spray with oil.
6. Pat salmon dry. Season with salt and pepper.
7. Transfer to pan, skin side down.
8. Brush with dill butter and lay lemon slices on top.
9. Roast until opaque. 12 - 17 minutes.

Variations:
Instead of dill, put Everything but Bagel seasoning or Furakake seasoning on salmon, add lemon slices, and bake.

Always try to extend grace and believe in the good intentions of your partner.

- Brent and Lauren Lewis, cousins

Honey-Glazed Chicken and Vegetables

By Brent and Lauren Lewis

Ingredients

2 lbs boneless, skinless chicken breast
3 medium potatoes, quartered
6 carrots, bias-sliced
½ cup honey
¼ cup prepared mustard
2 Tbsp olive oil
2 tsp curry powder
½ tsp garlic salt

1. In a large pot, boil potatoes and carrots for 10 minutes.
2. While boiling vegetables, in a saucepan, combine honey, mustard, olive oil, curry powder, and garlic salt. Bring to a boil, stirring constantly. Remove from heat; set aside.
3. Arrange potatoes and carrots around the chicken in a large baking pan. Spoon glaze over chicken and vegetables. Roast at 350° for 45 minutes; until chicken is no longer pink.

Serve with rice, if desired.

Marriage and cooking have some similar guidelines for success. One that I recommend is you don't need to measure. Meaning, in a marriage, don't keep score of who does how much or whose turn it is to do something. In marriage, you carry each other. Sometimes it's 50/50 on effort or who does what. Sometimes it's 80/20 or 100/0. Just do it. It will change, and you need to take care of and carry each other when your partner needs it. If you are measuring or keeping score, you are putting the effort into that and not into your partner. When you cook, you don't really need to measure 2 tsp of sriracha. Use what is right for you that day.
You will know!

- Korbi Carrison, a longtime friend of Robin and Brian, Robin's birthday turtle twin, and witness/moral support at Dina's birth

Egg Roll in a Bowl

By Korbi Carrison

Ingredients

1 lb ground beef or pork
1 teaspoon minced garlic
14 ounces shredded cabbage or coleslaw mix
1/4 cup low-sodium soy sauce, or liquid aminos
1 teaspoon ground ginger
2 teaspoons sriracha
1 whole egg
1 tablespoon sesame oil
2 tablespoons sliced green onions

1. In a large skillet, brown the pork or beef until no longer pink. Add the garlic and saute for 30 seconds. Add the cabbage/coleslaw, soy sauce, ginger, and sautee until desired tenderness. You can add a little water if you need more liquid to sautee the coleslaw down.
2. Make a well in the center of the skillet and add the egg. Scramble until done over low heat.
3. Stir in Sriracha. Drizzle with sesame oil and sprinkle with green onions. Add additional soy sauce and sriracha if desired.

This recipe yields 4 servings. Divide the pan in 4 to figure out the serving or weigh it and divide by 4. Weight will vary for each person that makes it depending on the brand or type of meat.

When I was younger living at home, friends of my parents (GG and Great-grandpa Jack) were over celebrating their 25th anniversary. Grandpa asked what the secret is for a long marriage.

The 'groom' replied, "Tolerance!"

We've laughed about that over the years, but ultimately it's true. You'll always love each other, but there will be things that bug you. And that's where tolerance comes in! 😊

-    Auntie Paula and Uncle Bill
Celebrating 50 years of marriage in 2023!

Pad Thai

By Paula Meier

Ingredients

8 ounces flat rice noodles
3 Tablespoons oil
3 cloves garlic, minced
3 Tablespoons fish sauce
1 Tablespoon soy sauce
5 Tablespoons light brown sugar (or regular if you don't have light)
2 Tablespoons rice vinegar
8 ounces uncooked shrimp, chicken, or extra-firm tofu, cut into small pieces

2 eggs
1 red bell pepper, thinly sliced
3 green onions, chopped
1/2 cup dry roasted peanuts
2 limes
1/2 cup Fresh cilantro, chopped
2 Tablespoons peanut butter (I like chunky!)
1 Tablespoon Sriracha, or more, to taste

1. Cook noodles according to package instructions, just until tender. Rinse under cold water.
2. Mix the sauce ingredients together. Set aside.
3. Heat 1½ tablespoons of oil in a large saucepan or wok over medium-high heat.
4. Add the shrimp, chicken or tofu, garlic and bell pepper. The shrimp will cook quickly, about 1-2 minutes on each side, or until pink. If using chicken, cook until just cooked through, about 3-4 minutes, flipping only once.
5. Push everything to the side of the pan. Add a little more oil and add the beaten eggs. Scramble the eggs, breaking them into small pieces with a spatula as they cook.
6. Add noodles, sauce, and peanuts to the pan (reserving some peanuts for topping at the end). Toss everything to combine.
7. Top with green onions, extra peanuts, cilantro, bean sprouts and lime wedges. Serve immediately!

Gratitude Practice
Every night before bed, tell each other
what you are grateful for. Do it even
when you're angry with one another.
Then, say "I love you," and kiss.

- Sheryl and Tom Freeman

French Toast

By Tom Freeman

Ingredients

Cinnamon bread
Eggs (1 for every two pieces of bread)
Milk
Vanilla
Butter
Maple Syrup
Berries and powdered sugar for garnish

1. Whip the vanilla, eggs, and milk.
2. Soak the bread to the point that it can't absorb any more.
3. Heat butter in a pan and sear the French toast on both sides.
4. Remove the French toast from the pan and cut it into cubes.
5. Heat more butter in the pan, and then place the cubes back into the pan, turning frequently
6. Be careful not to burn the butter, constant rotation.
7. Pour maple syrup over the cubes, while over medium heat, and constantly turn the cubes.
8. Remove from pan after consistency has changed to a sticky texture.
9. Garnish with powdered sugar and your favorite berries.

Black Pepper Chicken

By Sheryl Freeman

Ingredients

1 lb (450 g) chicken breasts (or thighs) , sliced against the grain into 1/4" (5-mm) thick pieces

Marinade
1 tablespoon light soy sauce (or soy sauce)
1 tablespoon Shaoxing wine (or dry sherry)
1 tablespoon cornstarch

Sauce
1/2 cup chicken broth
2 tablespoons light soy sauce (or soy sauce)
2 tablespoons Shaoxing wine (or dry sherry)
2 teaspoons dark soy sauce (or soy sauce)
1 tablespoon cornstarch
1 1/2 tablespoons sugar
2 teaspoons coarsely ground black pepper
1/8 teaspoon salt

Stir fry
2 tablespoons peanut oil (or vegetable oil)
1 tablespoon minced ginger
2 cloves garlic, minced
1/2 white onion, chopped
2 bell peppers, chopped (I used mixed colors)

1. Combine chicken, soy sauce, Shaoxing wine, and cornstarch in a medium-sized bowl.
2. Gently mix by hand until the chicken is coated with a thin layer of the mixture. Marinate for 10 to 15 minutes.
3. Combine all the sauce ingredients in a small bowl. Mix well and set aside.

4. Heat 1 tablespoon of oil in a large skillet over medium-high heat until hot.

5. Add the chicken. Immediately spread the chicken into a single layer using a spatula, with as little overlap as possible.

6. Sear for 30 seconds or so, until the bottom is lightly browned. Flip the chicken. Cook for 15 to 20 seconds. Stir occasionally, until both sides are browned but still a bit pink inside.

7. Transfer the chicken to a plate and set aside.

8. Add the remaining 1 tablespoon of oil to the skillet. Add the ginger and garlic. Give it a quick stir until fragrant.

9. Add the white onion and peppers. Stir and cook for 20 seconds.

10. Stir the sauce mixture until the cornstarch is dissolved completely, and pour it into the skillet. Stir with a spatula immediately and cook until the sauce thickens enough to coat the back of a spoon, a few seconds.

11. Add back the cooked chicken. Quickly stir a few times to coat everything with the sauce.

12. Turn off the heat and remove the skillet from the stove. Immediately transfer everything to a big plate so the ingredients won't keep cooking in the hot skillet.

13. Serve hot as a main dish.

Always communicate no matter what, and never go to bed angry. Kiss each other every time you leave the house.

- Kira Fiebig, Robins best friend growing up through high school

Homemade Bolognese
By Kira Fiebig

Ingredients

1 pound ground beef
1 pound ground turkey
1 pound ground (add your favorite pork, sausage, veal, etc.)
1 diced large onion
1 diced red bell pepper
2 diced carrots
Minced garlic cloves add as many as you like 2-10
2 TSBP Italian season
Pepper to taste
1 bottle of any wine
4 cups beef broth
1 large can tomatoes or tomato sauce (some people don't like the tomato chucks)
1/2 heavy cream
Parmesan Rind (if you but fresh save the rind for your sauce store in freezer)

1. In a large Dutch oven sauté onions, carrots, bell pepper, and garlic until onion and bell pepper is tender about 10-15 minutes
2. Add and cook ground turkey until done, next add your choice meat until done, then add ground beef. (I cook these in steps just to gain extra flavor as the turkey needs to absorb the most).
3. Add Italian seasoning and pepper (I usually don't add salt since there is enough in the beef broth and pasta when it's cooking.)
4. Next add your bottle of wine and cook it until it is basically cooked done to nothing this takes about 1/2 to 1 hour.
5. Add beef broth cook down to about half. If you have any chunks of Parmesan add that to sauce (I usually keep the rind from fresh cheese in the freezer just for this)
6. Add a large can of tomato sauce and then add heavy cream. Simmer for about 1/2
   Serve over your favorite pasta that was cooked in heavy salted water.

This makes a lot and I usually freeze quart-size baggies full for fast dinner nights.

Keep Communication Open... talk things out!

- Aunt Carole and Uncle Jerry (Lewis)
  Chicken Chili

Chicken Chili
By Aunt Carole

Ingredients

1 small yellow onion, diced
1 tbsp olive oil
2 cloves garlic, finely minced
2 (14.5 oz) cans low-sodium chicken broth
1 (7 oz) can diced green chilies
1 ½ tsp cumin
½ tsp paprika
½ tsp dried oregano
½ tsp ground coriander
¼ tsp cayenne pepper
Salt and freshly ground pepper, to taste
1 (8 oz) pkg Neufchatel cheese (aka light cream cheese) cut into small cubes
1 ¼ cup frozen or fresh corn
2 (15 oz) cans cannellini beans
2 ½ cups shredded cooked rotisserie or left-over chicken
1 tbsp fresh lime juice
2 tbsp chopped fresh cilantro, plus more for serving
Tortilla chips or strips, Monterrey jack cheese, sliced avocado for serving (optional)

1. Heat olive oil in a large pot over medium-high heat. Add onion and sauté 4 minutes. Add garlic and sauté 30 seconds longer.
2. Add chicken broth, green chiles, cumin, paprika, oregano, coriander, and cayenne pepper, and season with salt and pepper to taste. Bring mixture just to a boil then reduce heat to medium-low and simmer for 15 minutes.
3. Add Neufchatel cheese to soup along with corn and beans, and stir well. Simmer 5-10 minutes longer.

Desserts

Morning Glory Muffins
By Uncle Jerry

Ingredients

2 cups flour
1 ¼ cup sugar
2 ½ tsp baking powder
2 tsp cinnamon
½ tsp salt
3 eggs
1 cup vegetable oil
2 tsp vanilla
2 cups grated carrots
½ cup pecans (optional)
½ cup coconut
½ cup raisins
1 medium apple, peeled and grated

1. Combine first 5 ingredients.
2. Beat eggs and vanilla in another bowl. Stir into dry ingredients.
3. Fold in carrots, pecans, coconut, raisins, and apple.
4. Fill greased muffin tins. Bake 350 degrees, 20-25 minutes. Cool 5 minutes.

Laugh! It's ok to make fun of each other and always keep each other laughing. It's a recipe for success.

- Neil Popish (Former Godfather of Dina) and Jim Villela

Peach Farfel (Brian's Favorite)

By Neil Popish

Ingredients

2 large cans of sliced peaches
1 lb of matzo farfel
7 eggs
1 ½ cups melted butter or margarine
1 ½ cups of liquid peach juice
½ tsp salt
¾ cup sugar
Cinnamon sugar

Pour very hot water over the farfel and let drain. In a large bowl, beat eggs and add all other ingredients (except the peaches and cinnamon sugar). Pour half the mixture into a 9 x 13" pan. Spread half the peaches on top. Add 2nd half of the mixture on top and spread peaches on top. Sprinkle top with cinnamon sugar. Bake at 350 degrees for 60-70 minutes.

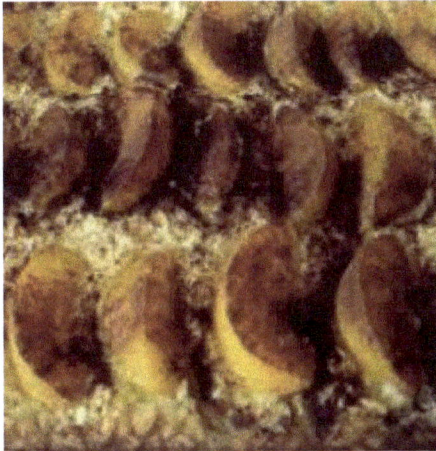

"LIFE is not about waiting for the storm to pass, it's about learning to dance in the rain."

- Linda & Sera Kelly

Food for the Gods

By Linda Kelly

Ingredients

1 ¼ cups all-purpose flour
½ teaspoon baking powder
½ teaspoon baking soda
¼ teaspoon salt
1 cup dates, pitted and chopped
1 cup unsalted butter, softened
1 cup white sugar
1 cup packed brown sugar
3 large eggs
1 cup chopped walnuts

1. Preheat the oven to 350 degrees F (180 degrees C). Grease a 9x13-inch baking pan and line it with parchment paper.
2. Whisk flour, baking powder, baking soda, and salt together in a bowl. Transfer 1/2 cup to a smaller bowl; add dates and toss to coat.
3. Cream butter, white sugar, and brown sugar in a large bowl with an electric mixer until light and fluffy. Add eggs, one at a time, beating well after each addition. Gradually stir in the flour mixture, then stir in floured dates and walnuts until well combined. Pour batter into the prepared pan.
4. Bake in the preheated oven for 10 minutes.
5. Reduce the heat to 300 degrees and bake until the top is dry and the edges have started to pull away from the sides of the pan. Approx 30 to 40 minutes.
6. Cool on a wire rack for 20 minutes before cutting into 36 bars.

Make sure you enjoy life together. Date nights and vacations are so important. Even with kids, you must find babysitters and go out on dates!

- Kate Harris-Golodner (friend of the family)

Harris Family Kugel Recipe

By Kate Harris

Ingredients

½ 6 ounce package egg noodles
3 eggs
½ cup of sugar
8 ounces (1 cup) sour cream
1 cup cottage cheese (small curd)
¾ cup milk
½ cup raisins
2 tablespoons butter (melted)
1 teaspoon vanilla
¼ teaspoon cinnamon

1. Preheat the oven to 350 degrees
2. Grease a baking dish with Crisco
3. Cook noodles and drain
4. In a bowl, beat the eggs and the sugar. Blend in the sour cream, cottage cheese milk, raisins, melted butter, and vanilla.
5. Add noodles to the mixture and then pour into the baking dish.
6. Sprinkle with cinnamon.
7. Bake for 1 hour

We wish you a marriage filled with lots of joy, love, and laughter. Be each other's cheerleader as you both continue to grow individually and as a couple.

- Cousins Steven and Julie Kahn

Chocolate-Covered Chocolate Chip Mandel Bread

By Julie Kahn

Ingredients

1 cup vegetable oil
1 teaspoon water
3 eggs
1 teaspoon vanilla
1 cup sugar

2 bags of chocolate chips
3 cups flour
cinnamon sugar
1 teaspoon baking powder
Nonpareils
½ teaspoon salt

1. Preheat oven to 350 degrees.
2. Blend eggs, oil, and sugar.
3. Add baking powder, salt, water, vanilla, flour, and 1 bag of chocolate chips.
4. Put dough on an ungreased cookie sheet in 2 rows-long thin logs (dough is sticky, wet hands).
5. Sprinkle with cinnamon sugar.
6. Bake at 350 degrees for 30 minutes.
7. Melt the other bag of chocolate chips and spread it over the warm Mandel bread.
8. Sprinkle with nonpareils.
9. Let the chocolate coating harden completely.
10. Cut into pieces.

People always used to say, and maybe
they still do,
"Don't go to bed angry."
That's a lot of pressure and I think it's
total garbage. Sometimes you're just
mad and it's time to go to bed. It's
okay to be mad at bedtime and work it
out in your own time.

- Susie, Ben & Morgan McCullough

EASY GOOEY CINNAMON ROLLS

By Susie, Ben & Morgan McCullough

Ingredients

1 package of frozen cinnamon rolls
1/2 cup white sugar
1/2 cup brown sugar
1 cup vanilla ice cream
1/2 cup butter

1. Place the frozen rolls into a greased 9x13 dish.
2. Mix all ingredients and bring to a boil on top of the stove.
3. Pour over the frozen rolls.
4. Let them rise for 8-10 hours.
5. Bake at 350 for 30-40 minutes.
6. Top with frosting packets that come with the frozen rolls.
7. Serve and enjoy!

As a couple, always shoot for happier.
You can only truly be happy when you focus on that for yourself.
As partners, your job is to make each other happier.

- Jenn Jenn

Snickerdoodle Cupcakes with Cream Cheese Frosting

By Jenn Jenn

Ingredients

2 Eggs, large
1 3/4 cups All purpose flour
3/4 cup Butter, unsalted
1 cup Cream cheese
1/3 cup Sour cream
2/3 cup Whole or low-fat milk

2 tsp Baking powder
1/2 tsp Baking soda
3 tsp Cinnamon, ground
1 cup Confectioners' sugar
1 1/8 cups Granulated sugar
1/2 tsp Salt
2 1/2 tsp Vanilla, pure

1. **Whisk together the dry ingredients**: flour, baking powder, baking soda, salt and cinnamon. Set aside.
2. **Mix the wet ingredients**: Beat sugar and butter until creamy, about 1 to 2 minutes. Add the eggs one at a time, beating well after each addition. Add the sour cream and vanilla, then mix just until combined.
3. **Alternate adding flour mixture and milk**. Add one third of the flour mixture and mix just until combined. Add half the milk mixture and mix again. Repeat, then finish with final third of flour mixture. Scrape down the bowl as necessary.
4. **Bake cupcakes**. Transfer batter to a muffin tin with paper liners. Sprinkle cinnamon sugar on top. Bake cupcakes at 350 F for 18 to 20 minutes. Cool completely before frosting.
5. **Make the frosting**: Beat butter and cream cheese until light and fluffy. Add confectioners' sugar and cinnamon and beat until combined, then mix in the vanilla.
6. **Frost the cupcakes**: Transfer frosting to a piping bag with desired tip. Frost cupcakes and garnish with cookie crumbles or a cinnamon stick.

In Turkish there's a saying that goes, "Let's eat sweet so we talk sweet."
In marriage or a relationship, the most important skill is communication skills in my opinion. Knowing how to listen and respond is the key.... And lastly as Rumi says, "Your heart knows the way. Run in that direction."

- Elmas

Puff Pastry Chocolate Balls

By Elmas

Ingredients

Puff Pastry
Chocolate bar (Dark or milk but I like it better with dark chocolate)
Oil
Powdered sugar

1. Thaw puff pastry at room temperature for about 15-20 minutes
2. Cut the pastry in squares
3. Place a square of a chocolate bar in the middle of the pastry and roll it into a ball
4. Deep fry them until golden
5. After cooling them for a few minutes, sprinkle powdered sugar all over

Don't just listen to your partner.
LISTEN to them.

- The Garfinkel Family

Garfinkel Family (Yogurt) Banana Cake

By The Garfinkel Family

Ingredients

½ cup butter or margarine, cut in chunks
1 tsp. baking soda
1 cup sugar
3/4 cup plain yogurt
2 eggs
1 tsp. baking powder
1 tsp. vanilla
2 cups flour
2 large bananas (very ripe)
1 cup chocolate chips (optional)

1. Use Steel Knife (food processor blade)
2. Process butter, sugar, eggs and vanilla for 2 minutes, scraping down bowl once or twice. Do not insert pusher in feed tube.
3. While machine is running, drop chunks of banana through feed tube. Process until blended.
4. Meanwhile, dissolve baking soda in yoghurt. Let stand for 1 to 2 minutes. Yoghurt will nearly double in volume, so use a 2 cup measuring cup.
5. Add to batter and process for 3 seconds.
6. Add chocolate chips to the flour (this is optional).
7. Add flour and baking powder to the batter. Process with 4 quick on/off turns, just until flour mixture disappears.
8. Bake in a greased and floured 9" square baking pan at 350°F for 50 minutes, until cake tests done.
9. Cool 10 minutes and then remove from the pan.

Freezes well.

Note: If baking in Pyrex dish, bake 10 minutes less. Yield: 9 servings.
Note: Sour cream may be substituted for yoghurt, if desired. Frost with Chocolate Cocoa Frosting.

CHOCOLATE COCOA FROSTING

Ingredients

2 cups icing sugar
4 tbsp. milk or hot water
4 tbsp. soft butter or margarine
1 tsp. vanilla
4 tbsp. cocoa pinch or two of salt
2 tsp instant coffee

1. Use Steel Knife (food processor blade) Add instant coffee to the milk.
2. Process all ingredients until smooth and blended, about 10 seconds.
3. Scrape down the sides of the bowl as necessary.

Note: The addition of instant coffee takes this icing to the next level.

www.ingramcontent.com/pod-product-compliance
Lightning Source LLC
Chambersburg PA
CBHW070828100426
42813CB00003B/539